Being Bartered For Sex (My Diary)

Being Bartered For Sex

D Caldwell

Being Bartered For Sex (My Diary)

Copyright © 2012 D Caldwell

All rights reserved.

ISBN-10: **0692132279**
ISBN-13: **978-0692132272**

Being Bartered For Sex (My Diary)

DEDICATION

I would like to dedicate this book my Lord and Savior, God! I pray every day for a change and a passion to do something I love. I feel a since of spark and excitement every time I talk about writing. I whole heartedly embrace this gift and will share my stories to the world. I have learned from my 13 year old daughter, J Caldwell that it is just has hard to write a fictional story as it is to write non-fiction. As a non-fictional story teller like my daughter, who poured her heart into her first novel, I had to dig deep into my fictional characters to bring them to live and relatable. My family is and will always be my inspiration, especially my beautiful and talented daughter and my loving husband, Eddie.

Being Bartered For Sex (My Diary)

Being Bartered For Sex (My Diary)

CONTENTS

	Acknowledgments	I
1	Introduction	II
2	What is Beauty?	Pg 6-11
3	Speaking Out Loud	Pg 12-15
4	Frustration	Pg 16-19
5	Fighting My Demons	Pg 20-21
6	My Relationship With Women…	Pg 22-24
7	Figuring Things Out	Pg 25-26
8	Tears	Pg 27-31
9	Before Therapy	Pg 32-34
10	Letting Go	Pg 35-43
11	A Sister's Love	Pg 44-49
12	Finding Peace	Pg 50-54
13	The Voice	Pg 55-58
14	Not the End -The Beginning	Pg 59-60
15	Happiness	Pg 61-64

Being Bartered For Sex (My Diary)

Being Bartered For Sex (My Diary)

ACKNOWLEDGMENTS

I would like all the poets and song writers in the world. The gift of a lyricists, storyteller, and artists who are able to capture the minds of users is powerful and undeniably genius.

Being Bartered For Sex (My Diary)

Being Bartered For Sex (My Diary)

INTRODUCTION

Hi, my name is Cassandra, and this is the story of my life. My journey will take you on an emotional ride. I have experienced some highs and lows from a young girl to womanhood. I have yet to understand how I survived entirely, but I did. I will take you through of maze of words and a scavenger hunt of emotions.

The pace will be riveting like air whipping through your hair as you speed on the NASCAR Raceway. Expect twists and turns from each stage of my life. I tread lightly with each incline, decline and near mishaps on the race to happiness. Sudden stops, head-on collisions, and the breath was taken out of me when I almost went over a cliff. The fast pace and quick gratification are what I was my life. However, I realize that I am traveling on roads, I never experienced before. Oh, how this is the test of my life! I can see the clouds thickening as I go closer to the mountaintop. The winding roads ahead are scary, but manageable. Reaching the mountaintop is a goal I imagine reaching. At that mountaintop is my happiness. Are you ready? Buckle up and get ready for the ride! LET'S GO!!

D Caldwell

You will have to determine which path I took to reach my world of happiness. Every poem and letter expresses my thoughts, emotions, and my state of mind I. Journaling is my therapy and here is the beginning of my story.

PROLOGUE

If someone had taught me that my body was my temple, what would life be like for me? I feel used, abused, lonely and sometimes dirty. Sex and prostitution are the oldest professions known to men. Sex has become my only means of livelihood. My erogenous appetite was on high alert until it became routine for me. Then numbness seeped in.

As a child, I watched my mother and my aunt give their bodies to men for cigarettes, weed or beer and alcohol. I learned all my tricks from them. I would hide in closets, behind walls or furniture to get a peek at them and listen to their conversations. I rolled my first joint when I was eight years old. I lost my virginity to one of my mother's boyfriends when I was 12. My youthful innocence was lost way before my virginity was taken from me.

I became rebellious, promiscuous and resentful towards my mother and my aunt. I was forced to move from home to home with the family who would take me in. I lived in and out of foster care for years. At some point, I remember my sister Simone was with me in and out of foster homes. Simone dated boys and girls. Simone was happiest when someone gave her false hopes and promises. Eventually, false hopes and promises became the force to make Simone her life. She put her head in her books; she joined ROTC.

Simone was the first and only one in my family to graduate high school. Simone was accepted into college and couldn't wait to leave! Simone vowed she would not live a lifestyle like this anymore and she will make something of her life.

I begin to ponder and ask questions like, why can't I change? I smile in pictures, but there is this disconnect. My family pushes me away because they think less of me. I experienced mental and physical abuse. I was raped and battered by an ex-boyfriend for two years. Drugs are my poison with some hard liquor to numb the pain. Anything strong, I do not discriminate! Weed and Cocaine are my prime choices! Whatever I have to do to get high, I will. Sometimes I make a cocktail out of the two drugs and take me to a zone that is unexplainable. The mixture of the two has put me out of commission for at least two days. Men are my future; they are my means of living. I have no job, no skills, and no diploma. What can a broke down drug addict whore do for a living, besides barter her body for her needs? I developed early, I have a banging body, but it has been used up, and I am only in my 20s. I will not reveal my age until later in the story.

Grown men willing to turn out young girls
Grown men with no morals
Grown men seeking sex & satisfaction
Grown men - don't know how to treat a woman - feel as though a young girl will accept anything.

I am getting older. Is there hope for me? Should I end my life in totality or should I stop my way of life? Who will help me? Where should I go?

My grandmother and grandfather have washed their hands of me. The best memories of my life were when I lived with my grandparents, but of course, I fucked that up royally. I have been to jail, the streets, foster care and group homes. I had STDs and some are permanent scars. Can I or will I find that man like Richard Gere in Pretty Women with Julia Roberts or does that only happen in movies? I want a family and children too. I know I can be a better mother than what I saw as a child. I love my mother dearly and my auntie, but damn!!! Why do I have to live like this???

Every year for my birthday I wish for something new. I am not talking about clothes or material things; I am talking about my life. Changes I must make. I don't know where to start. I don't know who to ask or who to trust. I can't even trust myself to make the right decisions. Look at how I turned out thus far.

I have emotionally bruised my ego and my inner self. My spirit seems lost, and my belief in a higher being is on shaky grounds. How and why would God want me to live like this? Do I have to go to church every Sunday to see results? Do I begin with prayer? Do I seek counsel from church or a therapist? Remember, I have no money, nothing but my body to give. I am too afraid to tell my sister, my baby sister what I am feeling inside. I don't have to reveal to her what I am going through, because she has witnessed it.

When my baby sister made that vow, that her life is more valuable than drugs and sex, I should have followed her. But, I didn't! Damn this life! I can't shake this devil or these demons.

Watch, I will grow, I will change, and I will prosper!
I am writing these thoughts and thinking aloud. By the end of this book, you will see the much-deserved changes I needed to make in my life.

D Caldwell

WHAT IS BEAUTY?

1 MIRRORED REFLECTION

I play the old childhood game of "Mirror, Mirror."

"Mirror, Mirror" on the wall, who is the ugliest of them all?

No answer, I am silent, I am numb.

"Mirror, Mirror" on the wall, who is the prettiest of them all?

No answer, I am silent,

I am numb.

What does this mean, I am not dumb

Nor will I succumb to society's beauty

I am braver than that, I know I am

Some say I am pretty and some say I am pretty damn ugly.

It will not define me.

No not me.

One day I will say, I am the prettiest of them all and believe the words as I speak them.

At this moment I believe I am ugly, but I was told by a wise person the definition of UGLY is:

Unique

Gifted

Loving

God loves you!!!

I CAN LIVE WITH THIS!! The question is do I believe it and accept it wholeheartedly??

2 WORDS DO HURT = LOW SELF-ESTEEM

Sticks & Stones may break my bones - but words never hurt...

LIES....... I say. All Damn LIES.....

I wonder who made this up?

Whoever thought of it?

Did they feel this way?

Those who have low self-esteem know better

Words are emotional or emotionless

Words have meaning or mean nothing at all

Words can hurt even the most secure person

Feelings are mixed emotions

D Caldwell

Emotions are feelings we have

Emotions are always described with words

Words become labels, stigma, piercing & gut-wrenching or bring joy & happiness!

Words are a powerful tool!

Words only hurt when they are used or spoken with malice intent.

Happiness and joy are what we yearn for wholeheartedly!

Words used from a slithering tongue or a ratchet hand displays hurt on anyone with feelings.

I will think before I speak, think before I write and think before reacting.

As I never want to be the one dishing out the hurtful words I received all of my life.

I seek and will speak true positivity!

My life. My spirit. I need cleansing from the hurtful words that have showered me.

PEACE! LOVE! LIFE! HAPPINESS!

These are words I will speak to my everyday existence!♥

SPEAKING OUT LOUD!

3 REFLECTIONS

Dear Cassandra,

Raise your head up and look in the mirror. You are smiling and laughing as you flip the pages of your grandma's photo album. You know, the photo album she told you not to take. You chose to ignore her and remind yourself; I may need this one day.

I slowly raise my head and, to my surprise I actually look happy. But, then I keep looking at the photos and notice my little sister, Simone is always out front smiling and I am in the back with a slight smile. I wonder why? Was I shy? Did I dislike taking pictures? Was that simply just my look? Not sure, but I remember we had lots of fun together.

I am coming to grips, each time I write a letter or poem, my sister is my saving grace! I don't want to distract her, but I need her so bad. Lord help me figure this out and ask for the help I need without disrupting her life.

I close the book and sit in silence, before drifting off to sleep......

Sleep has become my solemn peace.....

Love,
Cassandra

4 UNDER CONSTRUCTION = WORK AHEAD

Change is me. I am a work in progress!

My mind, body & soul are under construction

My mind is fed with spiritual thoughts

My mind is fueled by goodness

My mind is receiving information

My mind is processing this change

My body is nourished with healthy foods

My body is exhausted from strength building

My body is feeling & looking better already!

My spirit embodies my soul being uplifted

My soulful spirit continues to be challenged

Being Bartered For Sex (My Diary)

Construction is what it's called

I call it a life changing experience

Work ahead does not mean "Do Not Enter",

But enter with caution as the new me have a choice & a voice!

I will decide how I live

I will decide who I let into my space

I will decide who I will give my body to

Love me, love yourself and watch the reconstruction unfold into a work of beauty!

Peace ✌!!!!

D Caldwell

FRUSTRATION!

5 SORROW - PAIN - HUMILIATION

Dear Cassie,

What are you doing to yourself? Why are you doing this? Get up and face it head-on. You can stop. What about Simone and how she feels. I weep hard, and my chest begins to raise agonizingly up and down to the point I am having an asthma attack. I remember my inhaler is in my bag. I take two puffs, and I suddenly feel better. Temporary pain relievers. Temporary happiness. I need to reach out to the few friends I have left. I have pissed so many of them off, it is humiliating. I have slept with friends men and slept with the women too. I know you wonder how? Well I clean up pretty good and have a banging body. I have a fucked up attitude, mind and most of all -low self-esteem. I don't want to tell Simone, but she is the only soul in this world I trust. I need my little sister. I need help, terribly!!! I began to weep softly and soundly as I lay my pen down and doze off to sleep.....

Love,
Cassandra

6 THE STRUGGLE

What does "Struggle" mean to you?

Is it a task or goal requiring much effort to accomplish and achieve

-Or-

To advance with **"Violent"** effort

I identify with advancing with **violent** effort

Why use the word **violent**?

The struggle for me is intense and rough

I fight every day to pick myself up

It is a struggle to breathe, live, and exist in this world

I feel as though my mind is playing tug of war

Good vs. Evil fight every day

Some days Evil wins

Some days Good wins

Most days, numbness conquers all

I am a shell of a body that is empty inside

My soul has left my body

My morals are questioned every day

Yet God still loves me, because I have breath in my body

The struggle takes me in directions that are unparalleled with my healing

I stand outside this grandiose church every day deciding if I should go in or will

I just be another number in the congregation?

The struggle makes you question everything, including your faith!

I figure the first step to fighting the struggle is PRAYER!

D Caldwell

FIGHTING MY DEMONS!

7 ERRATIC THOUGHTS – THE WANDERING MIND

Dear Sandy,

How I crave for my next fix. I need the drugs and alcohol to soothe my lost and troubled ways. I need my Johns to pay for my habits. I sit here, clothes disheveled and my hair all over my head. I look around and notice the room is in disarray- especially the bed. The funny thing is, I don't remember a thing. Last night was a blur. How many times do I have to sell myself and my soul for a temporary fix? All I knows is when I get it; I am oblivious to anything that goes on around me. I like it. No worries or responsibilities. But wait, suppose if I get raped or damn, maybe I have been multiple times. I am just too fucking stupid to know and too damn high to remember. Oh my head is killing me. Damn it, Sandy, look at yourself and tell me what you see????

Love,
Cassandra

MY RELATIONSHIP WITH OTHER WOMEN......

8 SISTERS

My back hurt

I said my back hurt

Stilettos on my back

Knives & daggers in my back

The pressure of you standing on my back!!

Stop standing on my back to succeed

We should all walk together not separate!

Hold your sister up

Give her a helping hand

Don't use status as a cleaver

To chop me down to make you rise

Women need to support each other

Women need to uplift each other

We are fighting for equality with our men!

Stop & think before you belittle another woman!!

PAUSE…

This is my experience with my so called girlfriends

Once thought of as sisters

Betray starts – then this is the result!

FIGUIRING THINGS OUT…..

9 LETTER TO SELF – WHY???

Dear Cassandra,

As I wake up from a drunken stupor, my head is cloudy, and my vision is blurred. See, my friends call me "Cassie," but my John's call me "Sandy." I have no real true identity. I identify with three names and all my actions and personalities I portray crossover. Why am I so Damn confused? Help me Lord get my SHIT together. I can't do this by myself. I have to be one person and identify with my true self. It is exhausting living like this. Life in seedy hotels, motels or sleeping on sofas has to stop! I must shower to remove the stench of sex & drugs from my bodily form. I am not here. I seem to be floating and watching this mess of a life I have created. All I keep asking myself is why? Why, Why, Why??? What steps will I take to fix this? Only the Good Lord knows.

Love,
Cassandra

TEARS!

10 ANGER = HURT = PAIN

I am filled with rage, like a raging bull

Everything and everyone in my life is collateral damage

I swear I hit, I scream all in anger

I say hurtful things to people so they can feel my pain

It is true; misery loves company!

I use drugs and alcohol for comfort

We all know this is only a temporary fix

Why can't I let go and move on?

Why can't I get my life and get it right?

I hate feeling this way!

Anger and Hate are strong words

Anger and Hate are harsh feelings

When do I begin to heal?

What are the first steps of my healing process?

I feel as though my letters and poetry are therapeutic - but how long will it take for anger to dissipate?

Anger, hurt and pain, please leave me alone!

I cannot exist in this state of mind anymore!

I refuse to let anger take over my existence.

I will conquer this here anger and live, live, live!

11 CHANGING SEASONS = GROWTH

Changes in the seasons

Trees grow, and trees die

Trees shed their leaves for the new ones to bloom

The roots are the foundation of the tree

The trunk is its strength

The branches represent life's ventures

Leaves represent people

Flowers bloom in the Spring and create beautiful scents and colors to the backdrop of nature

I feel like leaves and flower petals are like the people in my life

They are only here for a season

I try to hold on

I try to feed, water and nurture them, but they still fall off

Is this a symbolic gesture of my life?

Will people come and go so fast and so quickly?

I often ask why?

I am told people come in your life for a season and a reason

I guess that's what I need to figure out

Who are the people that are deep-rooted with me and will be my supportive foundation?

Growth means maturity in nature, but not humans!

Maturity is learned behavior, through experiences and wisdom

We are groomed and nurtured, but not everyone agrees with everyone's caregiver

Humans fight, bicker, love, hate & disagree

But never nature, unless you count these natural disasters as natures angry moments

Teach me, guide me, LOVE-me. I want to grow and bloom into something beautiful. My spirit

DAMAGED, who will heal me?

As I sit under this beautiful tree, I feel

Raindrops fall on my face

I begin to get up, but I am frozen in my thoughts

Is this God's way of telling me to pay attention, open my eyes and see what life has in store for me?

Or is it just merely raining?

BEFORE THERAPY

12 THE BATTLE – BEFORE THE BREAK THROUGH

What is a Battle?

What is a Struggle?

Many call a battle a war

I call it a fight between good and bad

I have demons I fight everyday

I have goodness in me, I know I do

How do I conquer my demons and evil ways?

How do I rejoice after the battle is over?

Will there be physical scars or mental scars?

I am up for the challenge!

Good vs. Evil is the theme in my life – I am ready to erase!!!

I will chisel at his darken part of my life

Until a beautiful statue of humaneness is formed

I will proudly wear a badge of honor

That badge will be a glow of humanity and calmness

After the battle is won

The break through is captured

Reveal the new me!

I peel away layers of my past

Releasing the demons

Accepting the past

Remembering the past

Making the choice of how I live

Making the choice of my existence

Making moves in ways that gives me purpose and a chance

I am living my life my way!

I am living life on my terms!

Live! Live! Live!

LETTING GO!!!

13 HOLD ME – I RECEIVE YOUR SUPPORT

I scream, I yell and curse as I am embraced!

I am embraced with force and compassion

For I know not how to receive a helping hand

I am angry DAMN IT!

I am hurting all over with aches and pains

I do not know trust or trust anyone

I shake, shiver and sweat as I begin to detox

My truest supporters hold me up

My truest supporters take my abuse

They are here, but I am not

Why me? Why me?

Tears flow as I grit my teeth in angst….

Who are these people that are determined to help me?

They speak…..

We are here to help you

We are here to heal you

I listen, but I do not care

I am not there yet – not to receive support

Until the core break through

Finally I am here

I am able to say hold me

I say, "I receive your support and I am ready to heal"

Hold me! Hold me! I receive your support!

I speak these words as yell tirelessly and sob into my hands!

I sit up straight and firm and speak again….

I begin to yell those powerful words – I thought I would never speak

"I have to grips with my healing process"

I am not cognizant of my surroundings

I am in control of my actions

I have begun to release the toxins

I think, hear and see clearly

I have faced my demons and released my guilt!

I am on the road to recovery

I thank my truest supporters

I thank myself

The process continues and will never end

I am now a supporter

I too can hold the weak, leery and injured soul

Full circle has embraced me with Love, Comfort and Honesty!

Our undeniable supporters come in many forms

Often they are not those who are familiar to us

Sometimes they are those who know nothing at all about us!

14 Reach = Determination = Strength

I often wake up in cold sweats

Water pouring down my face

My body is soaked

I try to understand every dream

What they mean

I see myself climbing hills

Sometimes mountains

I fall every time I get near the top

My safety gear keeps me alive with the sudden drop from a mountain!

Then there are the water dreams

I am a great swimmer, but I keep drowning

Then there is a force that pushes me slightly above water where I began to breathe

What does this mean?

Are these triumphs I need to conquer?

Are these obstacles I must face and pass to before move to the next level?

Am I living my life in fear?

I am determined to succeed at every climb and every stroke!

Determination I will embody!

My Strength I will gain!

I will conquer whatever this is and become a force to be reckoned with!

Coming to Grips

Reality sets in as I look in the mirror

My stare is blank as tears stream down my face

My reflection reveals an empty soul and broken heart

I continue to stare at myself as I come to grips with my reality

I am sick, I am poor, I am hopeless, I'm an addict!

Coming to grips is risky watching it as it is speaking it

How do I conquer the illness that lives within me?

Coming to grips does not heal me

Coming to grips does not fix me

Coming to grips does not release the pain and hurt

But, coming to grips does make me realize that I need help!

It is up to me to ask for help before coming to grips dissipates and

I fall (deep swallow)……

Into (shallow breaths)…..

A downward spiral again!!!!

Acceptance

Acceptance is judgement

Many of us seek acceptance from others

Validation from others

Society makes the rules

But, do we all need to live by society's standards?

I am seeking acceptance within

I can't allow myself to be judged by others in seek of acceptance

I am judged every day and many of you don't know a DAMN thing about me!

Many of their presumptions may be right,

but does it make it right?

HELL NO!

I have to learn to accept my past, present and future

I have laid the ground work for my life through my ACTIONS!

I may have been influenced in many ways

I am taking my path back to rework it and set new ground rules as I begin

A new life…..

A journey of acceptance within!!!

A SISTER'S LOVE

My Sister's Story "Simone the Warrior"

Dear Simone,

Every picture, thought, emotion and illusion is worth a 1000 words. How very little did I know Simone was crumbling at the pieces? She was fighting her own demons while trying to stay strong for herself and me.

I knew Simone struggled with a few of her classes, but not to the point of failing. Simone vowed that failure was not in her vocabulary. Simone loved the school she attended and her new friends. But something went terribly wrong one night. I received back to back calls from Simone, but there was silence every time I answered. Then I received an inaudible voicemail from my sister where I only heard people in the background and faint sobs. I begin to ask my dear sister, "Are you okay?" Again there was dead silence. I am confused and I tell Simone, "Don't pull away from me now." "Let me be there for you, just as you were for me."

I later found out from a mutual friend of ours, that Simone was raped at party she attended off campus. Simone was distraught and was afraid to report the crime. Simone wanted to walk away with her head up high instead of walking in shame. However, what my dear sister failed to realize, she let the enemy win and take the life away from her that she worked so hard for.

Ultimately Simone, my dear sister dropped out of college and now works in the fast foot industry. This was not supposed to be her path or her journey. Together we must break this cycle and press forward. The torch is in my hand. I have to hold my sister up while we fight together.

I will help my sister re-enroll in college if it is the last thing I do. I am in a place where strength is everything and I am walking on solid ground. I have get her off of shaky grounds before she collapses and falls through. I will not allow that to happen. I have been there, my dear sister will not walk that path. Therapy first, the healing and then strength.

Two years later I sit in the audience of this huge arena surrounded by hundreds of people. I am proud of my sister, as I sit and watch her receive her Bachelors of Arts Degree in Sociology. My heart is full and my eyes are filled with tears. I am ecstatic at this moment. We did it Simone! Together, we did it! Powerful we are together and strength is our core force!!

Simone your story is a part of my healing process. I have to write this letter to you, to let you know I am here for you no matter what. We are each other's strength until we take our last breath. I love you Simone forever and always.

Writing has become therapy. I am able to read and reassess my life without trying to remember every detail, because I have already captured the details in my writings. This letter reaffirmation that anything is possible!

Love,
Cassandra

Sisterly Love

Simone guides me to rehab therapy

Simone's support and strength is my everything

Her words she speaks are music to my ears

I fight her every step of the way

She is frustrated, because she believes I am giving up

I hear her as she speaks

I can't fight the temptation

Simone yells in anger

I have never heard my sister raise her voice

This causes me to rise up and stand face to face with her

We lock eyes

I raise my hand

I am ready to smack the SHIT out of her!

Simone raises her hand and grabs my wrist

Simone speaks, "Not today, we don't fight"

At that sudden moment – I fell into my sister's arms

She held me tight and said, "I am hear for you sis"

We cried together…

Simone took me to my first therapy session

I walked out of many sessions

I told myself, nothing is wrong with me

My only saving grace was when Simone said this is it!

I saw the hurt and pain written on her face

I promised Simone this was it….

I will check in to a facility

This was the hardest thing I had to do

This was even harder for Simone to see me self-destruct

It wasn't apparent to me that my self-destruction would have a domino effect

My sister told me she love me everyday

I failed to do so, because my mind was always in a haze

Simone knew I loved her

Right?

After four weeks in this sterile facility, I was able to call my sister

I told her, "I love you sis"

Simone was silent

I knew she was smiling

I broke the silence

I said, "Stop smiling looking like cheesy face"

We both broke out in laughter

I hadn't laughed like that in so long

Laughter is good for the soul

Smiles makes for a pretty face and welcoming face

Positive energy is everything!

Simone and I kept in touch throughout my therapy

Sisterly Love is the best thing we share!

FINDING PEACE

Serenity = Water Dance = Precious Cargo

I gracefully sit on the Beach

I watch the currents in the water

Move from small ripples to waves

At times these waves burst into high tides

I watch the sun as it reflects on the water

And cast a beautiful stream of colors with

Reflections of the sun and the sky

I watch as boats wade through the waters

There are dinghy boats, fishing boats, sailboats and of course yachts!!

I think of myself as a dinghy - there is no flair or high demand for these boats

I dream of one day becoming a sailboat

The wind takes control, and the coxswain steers the boat, it is a battle of 2 forces, but the coxswain steers in the direction he so chooses

The conflict is arduous when there is a storm brewing, and the sea is angry - high tides thrust against the boats, ships, land and everything in its path!

I try not to think of this much

I look for the calm, serenity and peacefulness of the ocean and nature at it's best

The sailboat is wanted and desired by many

It is the next step up to a yacht

A yacht screams luxury, patience, style, hard work, success and makes a statement

My statement in life is the imprint of a dinghy

My future has the earmark of a yacht

I will persevere and become that most wanted and thought about individual

I will take pride in myself as the loving one I seek will nurture and take pride in me!

I am a dinghy first - I grow and become a sailboat - I blossom and become a grandiose yacht!

Freedom

Freedom has no burden

Like a bird, I fly free

Like a plane I soar through the sky

My flight is steady

It almost looks as though I am still

No movement unless you hear me

No movement unless you see my wings flap

Freedom is pure

Freedom comes at a cost

Freedom has breathed new life into my body

It was a hard fight to release my burdens

D Caldwell

It was a struggle to release with no regrets

I am free and I feel free!

Freedom is Me and I am free……

Being Bartered For Sex (My Diary)

THE VOICE

The Reveal – My last Struggle – "Cassandra speaks Truth & Wisdom"

Cassandra a bag of tricks

Cassandra had 3 identities

Yes, I said had!

Sandy, Cassie and Cassandra

I identify with Cassandra

Sandy and Cassie no longer exist!

My past is my story

My path is the beginning of my journey not the ending

I speak my truth

I don't play the run and hide game

What for?

Being Bartered For Sex (My Diary)

I am who I am

For I would not be who I am today if I had not walked

that faithful path

Love yourself first

Believe in the power of prayer

God is my saving grace

Reach others

Teach others

Respect others

Importantly respect yourself!

I have fallen in love with myself

I am a healthy 26 year old young woman with morals and

values

I fuel my body with energy and nutrition

Drugs, alcohol and unprotected sex does not feed my

soul anymore

Shed the tears if you need to

Yell if you need to

Journal if it helps

Seek help from your confidants

Seek help from therapists

Don't let therapy and psychiatry be a stigma of the black community

Use your resources to help you live a better life

Live for you and no one else

A better you, makes it better for the ones you love

A better you, allows you to love and receive love

A better you is the best gift in the world

My truth is valuable to me

My wisdom is sharable to all

I love me and I hope the messages here touched the hearts of all!

NOT THE END – THE BEGINNING

The Final Chapter

I stand in my bathroom wearing a simple blue silk gown, looking at the reflection of myself in the mirror. I begin to smile at what I see. I have started to love myself again. I am lost in thought at all that I have gone through to get here. Then I am startled out of my thoughts when I feel the strength of two strong arms wrapped around my waste. I couldn't stop smiling with the thought of happiness as a tear began to trickle down my face. My love, my new love wiped my tear and kissed me softly where the tear stain once was. His gentleness is so refreshing and unbelievable. I never knew love could feel like this.

This has been a journey and a voyage like no other. I must tell you how I met my king, my soon to be husband. The best way to do this is with a flow of words that will entangle your mind and spark your visualization of this remarkable transformation of Me!

Being Bartered For Sex (My Diary)

HAPPINESS!!!

D Caldwell

My Love - My King

Chance meeting or was it?

Our bodies simply grazed each other's with a simple passing by!

We locked eyes briefly

I felt my soul was being invaded

We smiled and walked away

Chance meeting or is it!

We crossed paths again

What is this or who is this?

Confusion sets in and so does fear

Is he following me or am I following him?

I walk away with a strut in my walk and a sway in my hips!

The thunder of his voice paralyzed my movement

I hear the words - "You are Simply Beautiful"

Being Bartered For Sex (My Diary)

I turn to meet this voice and became entranced in his gorgeousness

The old me would let lust take over

The new me is now patient and wiser

From that day on we talked purposely to feel and feed a need we both craved for!

Neither of us knew the cravings that were buried deep inside of us

The need for love and compassion is exhausting and exhilarating

I felt things in my loins I could not explain

This man - this chocolate man is making love to my mind - but how could this be?

Evocative words are spoken from his tender lips

My ears smile at the sound of his voice

My mind explodes with the words that massage every inch of my brain

His words are soothing

My responses grows in a manner unbelievable to me

I am changing before my very eyes

I learn as I speak - I read more - I have developed a sense of self

Where has this man been all my life?

My king - My Love has taught me the newness of life

I developed into a woman of substance and value before I met my king

Together we are enthralling each other's every thought through love, words & actions

We have yet to make love

It has been 6 months and we vowed to abstain from sex until marriage

Today is the day I will accept my vow in marriage to My Love, My King

Goodbye to my past and Hello to my future

My past I will never forget -

My future I accept!

Today is not the beginning of my new life

Today is the beginning of our union

Today I will become a Mrs.

I will not lose my identity

I will stand strong & wear my crown bestowed onto me as the Queen to my King!

Life Happens – This Was My Story!

ABOUT THE AUTHOR

D Caldwell is a new author on the rise. She chose her first novel to explore poetry through story telling. D Caldwell has found the girt to capture a story from a picture, an image or a subliminal thought. This story came to fruition just by looking at a picture. All the characters in this story are fictional, but rings true with anyone who is able to identify with any of the poetry or letters written in this book. Words have the power to be used in any given way and D Caldwell chose create a masterful piece of art!

www.ingramcontent.com/pod-product-compliance
Lightning Source LLC
Chambersburg PA
CBHW041945110426
42744CB00027B/12